Original title:
A Brooch in the Dark

Copyright © 2025 Creative Arts Management OÜ
All rights reserved.

Author: Rafael Sterling
ISBN HARDBACK: 978-1-80586-211-6
ISBN PAPERBACK: 978-1-80586-683-1

Whispers of the Night's Embrace

In twilight's hush, a giggle gleams,
A sneaky spark that dances, it seems.
The owls wear glasses, wise and spry,
While moonbeams wink and shadows fly.

Laughter reverberates through the trees,
While critters conspire with teasing ease.
They hide their treasures, mischief their art,
As fireflies twirl, a flirty part.

Treasures Veiled in Shadows

In corners dark, where whispers giggle,
A scampish light begins to wiggle.
A sock, a button, they're on display,
With stories to tell in silly ways.

A jaunty hat, a wayward shoe,
In the moonlight's glow, they come to view.
The misfits dance, so bold and bright,
Making the night a pure delight.

The Silent Spark of Remembrance

In stillness deep, a wink ignites,
Forgotten toys come out at night.
A rubber ducky, a teddy bear,
Plotting their pranks without a care.

They sneak and scurry, such playful cheer,
With little giggles only we hear.
A flash of color in shadow's tide,
Tales of the evening, all bonafide.

Glittering in the Depths of Night

Under starlit skies, a sparkle spins,
As laughter echoes, where fun begins.
The night is a trickster, bright and bold,
Its jewels of humor, a treasure to hold.

Each twinkle whispers a cheeky cheer,
As shadows gather, conspiracies near.
With a wink and a nod, the night takes flight,
In mischief wrapped, all wrapped up tight.

Glow Within the Quiet

In shadows where the giggles creep,
A shimmer hides, oh, what a peep!
It dances lightly, just for fun,
A spark that sparkles, one by one.

Amidst the gloom, a wink can thrive,
Like fireflies crash landing, alive!
Even the owls can't help but stare,
At this playful charm, so rare and fair.

A Radiant Keepsake of Dusk

Twilight falls with a cheeky grin,
A treasure tucked, let the jest begin!
It winks at stars with a mischievous glee,
Whispering secrets for you and me.

Laughter flits with the evening breeze,
While shadows huddle, the humor frees.
Each chuckle glimmers, bold and bright,
In this jolly jest, the dark feels light.

Jewels Beneath the Moonlight's Caress

Little gems, under moon's sweet touch,
Giggling softly, oh, such and such!
They sway and twinkle, a playful lot,
In midnight's circus, they share a spot.

A laugh-out-loud from the heavens' face,
Hiding in corners, they found their place.
Every chuckle spins, a shining dance,
In this cleverly crafted moonlit romance.

Hidden Gleams of the Night Sky

Starlit giggles in the velvet blue,
Tiny treasures, peeking through.
They wink and nod, enjoying the show,
As night slips in with a gentle glow.

Frolicsome whispers on the cool night air,
A sparkle here and a twinkle there.
With mischief in tow, they plot and scheme,
Creating humor like a silly dream.

Glimmers of the Unheard Night

In shadows where the giggles creep,
A glow begins, no need for sleep.
A wink from stars that wink just right,
They dance and tease, oh what a sight.

The raccoons plot a midnight feast,\nWhile owls hoot
jokes, they're quite the beast.
Glimmers of mischief in the air,
While nothing stirs, yet all is there.

In the thick of dark, they break and play,
The moon snickers, lighting their ballet.
With whispers soft, they scheme with glee,
What a ruckus in total spree!

So if you find yourself alone,
Look for the spark, it's widely shown.
For laughter hides in every nook,
Just peek, and you'll see how they look!

The Beauty That Lurks Beyond Nightfall

When the world winks into a limbo,
Creatures gather, a glowing bingo.
With glittered tails and moonlit eyes,
They chant and cheer beneath dark skies.

The cats concoct their daring plans,
High fives exchanged among the clans.
Fireflies serve drinks from tiny jars,
As hedgehogs judge their dancing stars.

A rabbit juggles with wild flair,
While bats in capes swoop through the air.
The beauty shines, in every bark,
As laughter echoes in the dark.

So join the fray and lose your mind,
In midnight's glee, true joy you'll find.
Embrace the whimsy, shed your fright,
For fun awaits in the cloak of night!

Pieces of Light in the Abyss

In the depths where silence hums,
A glow appears, oh how it drums.
Mice in tuxedos spin around,
While crickets chirp a jazzy sound.

Invisible friends, they play charades,
In the dark where laughter fades.
A fox in glasses reads a map,
With every turn, they flip and clap.

A treasure hunt without a care,
For shiny bits that dance in air.
The tin can traces lead the way,
To silly dreams that come to play.

So wander near the velvet black,
Where humor hides and thoughts are slack.
Collect the glimmers, one by one,
In the abyss, the fun's begun!

Secrets in a Shroud of Midnight

In the silence, secrets bloom,
As night unfolds its playful room.
Shadows shiver and softly hum,
A cheeky grin, the night's just begun.

The sun has gone, the stars take charge,
While owls recite lines, quite large.
Hedgehogs wear hats, it's quite absurd,
As whispers share the silliest word.

Ghosts with giggles, stealing treats,
In the night their mischiefs greet.
With every laugh, a moonlight chase,
In this shroud, there's a merry place.

So come along and spill your fears,
Join the night, release your cheers.
In the dark's embrace, find your spark,
Dance with secrets till it's stark!

A Jewel's Journey Beyond Light

In shadows deep, it winks and beams,
Crafted by laughter, woven with dreams.
Oh, what mischief, it seems to say,
Dancing through night, in a playful ballet.

With crystals bright that twinkle and tease,
It tickles the air, puts worries at ease.
From closet corners to gleaming displays,
This jewel rocks wonder in comical ways.

Enigmatic Charms of the Nocturnal

A charm that giggles in moonlight's grace,
Whispers of secrets in a sparkling space.
Each twinkle a jest, a playful delight,
Beneath the stars, it spins through the night.

With every flicker, it shares a grin,
A glint of mischief as it draws you in.
In shadows it winks from a nearby tree,
"Join in the fun, come dance with me!"

Illuminated Whispers of the Unknown

A shimmer of laughter in places unseen,
Glowing with giggles, the night is bright green.
In corners of chaos, it finds its scene,
Telling tall tales that are light and serene.

The darkness may murmur, but this gem will shout,
"Who needs the sun when I've got this clout?"
With each playful flicker, bringing delight,
It turns every shadow into sheer sunlight.

Traces of Wonder in the Obscurity

In the deepest of dark, a sparkle appears,
Tickling the silence with boisterous cheers.
It rolls with the giggles, skips with the bliss,
A treasure that glimmers, oh, what a twist!

From nooks and crannies to grand masquerade,
This playful little gem isn't afraid.
It laughs at the night, with a cheeky spark,
Creating its magic from shadows so dark.

Embers of Distant Memories

I stumbled on a thought today,
A tale of socks that went astray.
One vanished in the wash, oh dear,
To hide beneath the couch, it's clear.

The cat sits smug, a quirky king,
With missing yarn as his new bling.
I wonder if they share a laugh,
My socks and feline's mischief craft.

A dance of memories through the haze,
Of mismatched pairs in youthful days.
Like embered stories in a stack,
Unraveled threads that giggle back.

Though time may steal my clouded sight,
That sock will always bring delight.
A warmth in wool, a spark anew,
In every stitch, a laugh rings true.

Jewels Beneath the Moonlight

Beneath the moon, a stash of fun,
Old toys and trinkets, everyone.
A rubber chicken, bright and proud,
It honks and quacks, out loud, out loud.

A sparkly ring from days of yore,
It once adorned my cousin, poor.
Now it sits, a relic bright,
A treasure lost in homemade flights.

With giggles shared and stories spun,
A gathering of artifacts begun.
Each jewel a giggle wrapped in night,
An heirloom's laugh, a silly sight.

The stars above twinkle, tease,
As laughter rides upon the breeze.
In shadows play, the memories spark,
As laughter lights the ever-dark.

Radiance Entwined with Silence

In quiet corners, whispers stir,
An old lamp flickers, it might confer.
With dusty bulbs that hum and sway,
A glow that mocks the end of day.

The teapot sits in regal pose,
With tales of tea that's long since froze.
Once filled with dreams and tasty brews,
Now just a haunt for pesky snooze.

The carpet bears the weight of cheer,
A dance of crumbs from yesteryear.
As laughter tumbles down the hall,
In silence, echoes build a wall.

Yet in this glow, the giggles bloom,
A room of joy breaks through the gloom.
With every shadow, every glance,
A radiance found in this old dance.

Shadows of Gilded Dreams

In shadows where the dreams all play,
A golden fish now swims away.
With fins of sparkles, teasing light,
It flops and flails, a comical sight.

The frog upon the lily pad,
Croaks tales of life, oh isn't that rad?
His crown of leaves, a regal scheme,
In stillness, he casts a silly dream.

The moonlight shines on every jest,
On whimsy's treasure, it takes a rest.
In gilded hues, the chuckles sneer,
As laughter hangs in evening's sphere.

In whimsical worlds where shadows gleam,
Life's a parade, an endless dream.
With every hop and playful swirl,
The funny side of dusk unfurls.

An Adornment's Solitude

In shadows deep, a gem does sigh,
Alone it sparkles, asking why.
It peeks from pockets, looking grand,
Yet no one cares, it understands.

Each evening drags, no hand in sight,
It wonders, will it shine tonight?
A lonely glimmer, just a tease,
With all its shine, it longs for ease.

Echoes in the Twilight

In twilight's glow, a wink is shared,
The laughter follows, unprepared.
A little stone, against the light,
Winks at the moon, a funny sight.

With twinkling eyes, it starts to dance,
In shadows deep, it finds romance.
No one can see the fun it has,
Just waiting for a night-time pizzazz.

Luminous Secrets Wrapped in Night

Secrets sparkle, tucked away,
In crevices where shadows play.
A mismatched pin, quite out of place,
Giggles softly, joins the race.

With a twist, it pulls a prank,
On sleepy bugs, it gives a rank.
Who knew a trinket held such glee?
In moonlit scenes, it roams so free.

The Enchantment of Hidden Charms

Amidst soft whispers, charms collide,
They chat and giggle, oh what a ride!
A hairpin snickers, a clasp joins in,
Creating mischief without a grin.

They hide in drawers, they plot and scheme,
To jump in bags, a jeweled dream.
At parties shy, they play the part,
Secretly crafting their own art.

In the Embrace of Obscured Light

In shadows where mischief creeps,
A spark of humor slowly peeps,
Glimmers from pockets, quite absurd,
Whispers of laughter, ever heard.

When darkness falls with a cheerful grin,
Balloons and bubbles twirl within,
A wink from the moon, a playful tease,
Jests that dance on a gentle breeze.

Frogs wear hats, and cats sing tunes,
As radiance plays amid playful ruins,
A glow that tickles the air around,
In every giggle, lost treasures found.

So let us prance through night's delight,
Collecting giggles in soft moonlight,
For in this gloom, joy's not so stark,
Life's little quirks ignite the dark.

Hidden Charms of the Nocturnal Realm

Hidden treasures on a starry night,
Bats in top hats take a flight,
Fairies giggle behind a tree,
Hiding trinkets—come and see!

With jesters capering, oh so spry,
Catching dreams as they float by,
While owls recite poems of fear,
In this silly world, we cheer!

The stars are winking, don't you know?
Invisible unicorns put on a show,
Slippers made of clouds take a leap,
As laughter sparks the night from sleep.

So join the fun, don your disguise,
As shadows mix with moonlit sighs,
For in this mirth, with charming glee,
Our keen hearts dance in jubilee.

Mystical Jewels of Silhouette

In the stillness, secrets gleam,
A wink and nod—a playful dream,
Where sleepy critters scamper by,
And silly shadows humorously fly.

A glint of mischief, absurd and rare,
Sparks of giggles dance in the air,
Tickled by whispers of the night,
Enchanting charm in delight's light.

With hats that twirl and shoes that squeak,
Even the bushes begin to speak,
As creatures of whimsy come alive,
In this realm where oddities thrive.

So gather 'round, embrace the odd,
For it's the laughing that we applaud,
In moments lost and giggles found,
The nocturnal gems do astound!

Echoes of Enchantment in the Dimness

Amid the murmur of quiet night,
A cast of characters takes their flight,
Glowworms twinkle, like shiny gems,
As laughter echoes in silly hems.

Balloons and bubbles, whispers of cheer,
While shadows jiggle without fear,
The charms of night, a whimsical play,
Every dark corner leads us astray.

Unseen friends in a frolicsome glow,
Dancing figures in a splendid show,
With every giggle that stirs the air,
A tapestry of fun lies everywhere.

So let's weave tales of joy and delight,
In the sleepy world of the starry night,
Where each chuckle and silly spark,
Turns dimness into a whimsical arc.

Starlit Trinkets of the Soul

In shadows where giggles bloom bright,
A shining pin takes its playful flight.
It twinkled with each silly dance,
Spirit of whimsy, a chance romance.

Sparkles of laughter, a comic show,
Chasing the gloom, let the mirth flow.
With every twirl, a chuckle does spring,
The night's little treasure, oh what joy it can bring.

Hidden glimmers from a costume box,
Adorning the night like laughter's flocks.
Each piece whispers secrets it knows,
As they frolic around, with mischief they pose.

A jester's wink in the depths of the night,
This gaudy gem surely feels just right.
With winks and nudges, it steals the scene,
A laugh in the dark, oh, what a routine!

The Veil of Forgotten Jewels

Behind curtains of laughter, they tease,
Forgotten treasures, they aim to please.
Dusty wonders in a whimsical round,
Charmers of smiles where silly joys abound.

A rogue's delight, a tangled mess,
This collection of jests wears its best dress.
Each spark of humor, a tickle on lips,
Witty little wonders, in the world's clips.

Veils of laughter delightfully sway,
Every old jewel has something to say.
Entwined in giggles, the stories unfold,
Sparkly humor that never gets old.

With every shine, a memory reigns,
Of quirky times and silly pains.
These forgotten jewels in laughter's embrace,
Lift the spirit, grant life a pace.

Echoes of Radiance in the Dark

In the still of the night, whispers do glide,
A shimmer of humor where shadows collide.
Beneath the surface, a grinning spark,
Radiates joy in the corners so dark.

Jokes fly like fireflies, lighting the gloom,
With each little giggle, the night's in full bloom.
A flicker of starlight, a playful wink,
Echoes of laughter on the edge of the brink.

A treasure map drawn by a comic hand,
Leads to the brightness of a whimsical land.
Tales of the silly and sparkles of fun,
In the depths of the night, we dance 'til we're done.

As echoes of radiance twirl 'round and around,
We're wrapped in the humor, together we're bound.
So let's toss in some giggles, let's break out the cheer,
In the dark, we find brilliance, oh, how we endear!

Luminous Dreams of the Unseen

Glittering secrets in shadows they weave,
Luminous dreams that make us believe.
Giggles that giggle in corners they hide,
Whispering fables that come out with pride.

A collection of wishes that twinkle at night,
Catching the heart like a jovial kite.
Those whimsical pieces that sparkle and tease,
Dancing with laughter, they aim to appease.

Joyful antics in a mischievous game,
Conjuring smiles, we'll never feel lame.
A sprinkle of humor from unseen places,
Enlightening all with the best of their graces.

So gather the laughter, let's share and decree,
In luminous dreams, all hearts are set free.
With glimmers of joy, our spirits uplift,
In the playful shadows, we find our true gift.

Secrets of the Starlit Veil

In shadows where whispers play,
A crowbar of secrets hides away,
While owls wear monocles, quite absurd,
And gossip with squirrels, quite unheard.

The moon winks with a mischievous grin,
As stars engage in a dance akin,
To a party of fireflies, dressed in glows,
Debating the fashion of nocturnal clothes.

Dandelions chuckle in the night breeze,
As crickets compose symphonies with ease,
Each laugh echoes through the velvet dark,
Where mischief ignites like a tiny spark.

So let the night bring its giggling jest,
With secrets that twinkle and never rest,
For laughter's the key to unlock the fun,
In this whimsical world where we all run.

Forgotten Gems of the Evening

In a pocket of dusk, where oddities play,
A sock shines bright, in a magical way,
While toasters debate which crumbs are best,
And moths in tuxedos host a grand fest.

A chandelier made of jellybean trees,
Dances with shadows, swaying with ease,
Laughing at whispers of forgotten sights,
Where time slips on banana peels every night.

The stars wear pajamas, cozy and warm,
While clouds join the circus, all sweet and charm,
As echoes of laughter blend with the dark,
Creating a symphony, a delightful lark.

So cherish the gems that flicker and blend,
In the pockets of evening, where dreams never end,
For humor is hidden in shadows divine,
Amidst the forgotten, where stars brightly shine.

The Enigma of Midnight's Kiss

At midnight, the clocks all start to giggle,
As shadows twist and start to wiggle,
While cats in top hats ponder their fate,
In a riddle of moonlight, they dance and skate.

The stars exchange secrets in hushed tones,
While the grass tickles feet with its soft moans,
Jellybeans roll down the starlit street,
Where laughter erupts, oh what a treat!

Wondrous balloons float in shimmering air,
Winking at secrets that float everywhere,
As mischief spills forth like a fizzy drink,
Encouraging minds to giggle and think.

So lend an ear to the night's playful bliss,
In a swirl of twinkling, a midnight kiss,
For hilarity lurks in each nook and turn,
In the enigma of laughter, let dreams burn.

Elegance Lost in the Gloom

In the gloom where elegance takes a trip,
A monocle penguin performs a flip,
While dress shoes argue with sneakers in fun,
Debating the merits of shimmer and run.

Velvet mice tiptoe with grace so sublime,
Waltzing with shadows, dancing in time,
As bats wear top hats and croon a tune,
Under the gaze of a sleepy moon.

A chandelier giggles with each little sway,
As laughter finds echoes, lighting the way,
So lost in the charm of the night's gentle hum,
Where elegance stumbles and welcomes the fun.

In the embrace of the night's warm caress,
Comedic chaos becomes the new dress,
For in every shadow and whispered refrain,
Is elegance lost in laughter's domain.

Beauty We're Yet to Discover

In a drawer, where odd things hide,
A treasure waits, with a sense of pride.
A sparkly thing that squirrels would boast,
   Yet it's just a paperclip, not the most.

When socks are lost and secrets sprawl,
It twinkles at me, "Come give a call."
I let out a laugh, a giggle or two,
Who knew a paperclip could wear so blue?

Last year's junk turned to posh delight,
Like finding a diamond in the lap of night.
I ponder its worth in the grand scheme of things,
Then realize its glory is just what it brings.

So here's to the oddities tucked away tight,
In corners of cupboards, they share their light.
A beauty disguised with modest attire,
Makes the mundane feel like it's meant to inspire.

Glittering Silence of Unfathomable Night

Beneath the stars that twinkle and tease,
A cat's midnight joy, a gentle breeze.
Oh, the glittery stuff that falls from the trees,
Turns out to be dust, as I sneeze.

In this silence where shadows hide,
Crickets sing a tune, but never quite guide.
The treasures I seek in the moon's soft glow,
Are just old coins, as if made from dough.

Each shimmer's a giggle, a whispering joke,
What sparkles at night? Why, it's just some smoke!
Yet I dance 'neath the sky, in my mismatched shoes,
Turning the dark into glorious hues.

So gather your gems, the quirky and sweet,
For laughter in night is a charming treat.
With each piece of glitter, let fun be the spark,
In the cacophony of a silvery dark.

A Dazzling Enigma Beneath the Starlight

In the garden, where shadows prance,
An odd little gem puts me in a trance.
Is it a beetle or a lost piece of flair?
With all of my guesses, I'm left in despair.

The owls hoot loudly, with curious pride,
As I scribble down thoughts, feeling bonafide.
But that little sparkle? It dances away,
Like it knows I'm here, asking it to stay.

Maybe it's magic or just a crush,
On a daisy's heart, I feel quite the hush.
As laughter erupts from the leaves overhead,
I resolve to embrace all the chaos instead.

So cheers to the wonders that tease and delight,
Those odd little mysteries hidden from sight.
I'll treasure this chase, with every strange wink,
For joy lies in laughter, so what do you think?

Tales of Forgotten Gemstones

Once upon a time, in a land full of dreams,
Lived jewels that jiggled with bright, silly beams.
They'd gossip and giggle, making quite a fuss,
But where are they now? Just a layer of dust.

A sapphire who snorted, a ruby with flair,
An emerald that sneezed, oh how they would scare!
We'd gather them 'round for a wild little show,
But life got too busy, and off they did go.

Now tales of these gemstones drift softly like smoke,
Meritless memories, a farcical cloak.
Yet still I remember those whimsical nights,
When laughter would echo beneath twinkling lights.

So here's to the stories that float in the air,
Of goofy old gems that are no longer there.
For even in absence, their joy still remains,
In our hearts, their spark will dance like the rains.

The Serene Glow of Forgotten Objects

Beneath the couch, a shiny spoon,
Hiding where it heard a tune.
A rubber duck with quite a grin,
Checks its watch, wonders where to begin.

Dust bunnies waltz on borrowed time,
They twirl in rhythm, it's quite sublime.
Once forgot, now they steal the show,
Under the glow of a fridge's low glow.

Old coins clink as they start to sing,
About the joy of a lost, odd fling.
They dance like stars in a forgotten jar,
Reminding us of how weird we are.

A sock appears, its partner a ghost,
Together they wiggle, it's quite a boast.
They whisper secrets of laundry day,
While giggling about the games they play.

Dreams of Glow in Enigmatic Depths

In the depths of a drawer, a crayon sleeps,
Dreaming of rainbows, their colors in heaps.
A paperclip wishes it could take flight,
Twisting and tumbling, oh what a sight!

Forgotten erasers plot their escape,
From the grip of a pencil, oh what a caper!
They giggle and snicker, with plans to deceive,
Daring the ruler to make them believe.

A sticky note whispers, 'I'm here for fun!'
With doodles of sunshine, it glows like the sun.
Together they hatch a mischievous scheme,
To paint the old desk with a wacky dream.

While buttons plot mischief, they roll in a line,
Trying to hitchhike to a party divine.
Amidst all the chaos, they chuckle from out,
Life's hilarity hidden, without any doubt.

Celestial Embers of the Night

A candle burns with a cheeky grin,
Winking at shadows that dance within.
A sock puppet flickers, with laughter unbound,
Dreaming of stardust lost and found.

The moonlight giggles, a sly little tease,
Throwing sparkles on branches with ease.
Fireflies flicker, like tiny lights,
Having a party on warm summer nights.

A lonely shoe bops to an unseen beat,
Tapping its sole, it's quite the feat!
It sings to the stars, quite out of tune,
Claiming the night as its own cartoon.

With cosmic confetti that twirls in the air,
The world's just a stage when you dare to dare.
Laughter erupts as we twirl and sway,
To the rhythm of night, in a silly ballet.

Echoes of Light Wrapped in Darkness

In the shadows, a flashlight beams,
Waking up echoes of old dreams.
A cat in the corner rolls its eyes,
Chasing the light with silly surprise.

A teacup giggles, with saucer in tow,
Spilling its secrets, just letting them flow.
Nearby, a gnome with a wink and a grin,
Whispers to crickets, 'Let the fun begin!'

Under the bed, a monster just plays,
With socks and lost toys, all in a haze.
It roars with laughter, but not out of fright,
Just hoping for friends to join in the night.

When shadows unravel the mysteries found,
We laugh at the silliness all around.
For every dark spot has stories to spin,
Wrapped in delight, where the fun will begin.

Treasures Unseen in Velvet Nights

In pockets deep where secrets hide,
A button sparkles, though I lied.
It's not a diamond, just some flair,
Yet makes my jacket quite a scare.

With every twinkle, laughter blooms,
Beneath the stars, in darkest rooms.
A silly gem brings jokes to play,
As shadows dance and night turns gay.

Plucked from the sofa, lost and found,
It dangles proudly, oh-so-round.
Each twirl a giggle, each wobble cheer,
In velvet nights, the fun draws near.

So grab your pals and take a look,
At all the treasures none mistook.
For charm is found in oddest things,
And joy, my friend, is what it brings.

The Luminous Heart of Shadow

In shadows thick where giggles dwell,
A shiny heart begins to swell.
Though it's just plastic, painted bright,
It glows with charm and pure delight.

With every flicker, stories burst,
Of playful jest and laughter first.
These silly trinkets in the gloom,
Transform the night into a room.

A necklace made of bottle caps,
Unites us all with silly claps.
We share our fears, our dreams so bold,
With every glimmer, laughter told.

So here's to shadows that amuse,
With hearts aglow, we cannot lose.
In every laugh, a joy ignites,
Our luminous fun in velvet nights.

Glowed Trinkets of Twilight Tales

In twilight's grasp, the stories start,
With glowed trinkets that catch the heart.
An old dime shining in the breeze,
Whispers merry nothings with ease.

A quirky charm that's bright and round,
In every heart, a giggle found.
Beneath the moon, these tales unfold,
With every story, the laughter's told.

From mismatched socks to silly hats,
We wear our joy like playful chats.
And every trinket, tossed in gloom,
Transforms the room, makes friendship bloom.

So gather close and share your find,
With every laugh, we're intertwined.
For in the dark, the fun's a spark,
Glowed trinkets lead adventures' arc.

A Hidden Story Adorning the Night

In secret nooks, where shadows cling,
A curious tale takes joyous swing.
An earring lost, now on display,
A cheeky grin lights up the way.

It shines like stars, though it's so small,
We giggle, whisper, 'Is that all?'
Yet in its charm, we find delight,
As stories bloom in secret night.

A quirky badge from long ago,
Reveals the tales of highs and lows.
With every glimmer, laughter soars,
As hidden stories open doors.

So here in night, let joy ignite,
With treasures hidden from our sight.
Each little twinkle has its claim,
Adorning us with laughter's flame.

Glints of Memory in the Shadow's Fold

In twilight's clasp, a wink was cast,
A tale of laughter, memories fast.
With whiskers twitching, a cat in flight,
Chasing shadows that giggle at night.

Beneath the moon, a dance commenced,
A playful heart, nowhere tense.
Jokes whispered low, in gentle hues,
As echoes of joy, played their ruse.

Stars above winked in delight,
A tapestry spun, so feather-light.
With every footfall, a secret shared,
In the dim-lit world, none were scared.

So gather 'round, with smiles in tow,
In darkness found, let the good times flow.
Adventures abound, with laughter's spark,
In memory's folds, we leave our mark.

Secret Radiance of the Hidden

Beneath the bed, a treasure spree,
Old game pieces, missed by thee.
Dust bunnies dance, a sight to see,
Whispers of chaos, wild and free.

In closets deep, a shoe's a hat,
Nonsense rules, how silly is that?
Jumbled hints of what was lost,
Hidden gems at a comical cost.

Along the shelves, lost socks unite,
A party bright in the dead of night.
Laughter erupts, who'll find the match?
Radiant secrets, never a catch.

So tiptoe light, with giggles tight,
In hidden corners, find your light.
Together we dwell, in this merry arc,
Seeking joy in shadowed spark.

The Unseen Gleam of Starlight

In corners dark, where odd socks dwell,
A story blooms, oh can't you tell?
Squeaky toys and whispers low,
A secret club, where giggles grow.

Underneath the couch, what a sight,
Glittering crumbs in the dreamy night.
A pickle jar, full of lost dreams,
Shining bright with mischievous beams.

With stars above, we plan our spree,
Unseen laughs, just you and me.
In hidden paths, let's take a chance,
As shadows jiggle in a wild dance.

We'll toast our luck with lemonade,
In a world so bright, who needs a parade?
The unseen gleam, we'll chase it down,
In laughter's realm, we'll wear our crown.

Luminescence in the Depth of Shadows

In the nook where the old shoes lie,
A twinkle blooms, oh my, oh my!
Mice plotting, with plans so slick,
In darkness, they move with a comedic trick.

Beneath soft blankets, giggles hide,
A world of whimsy, where fun collides.
With whispering tales in wobbly tones,
This shadowland feels like home.

Come join the game of the unseen kind,
With laughter echoing, gently unwind.
In every crevice, a story beckons,
In the silliness, no one reckons.

So toss your worries—let the fun restart,
In luminosity found, we find our heart.
In shadowed corners, bonds we sow,
Together we thrive, in this joyful glow.

Secrets We Wore at Dusk

In twilight's glow, we don our charms,
With winks and giggles, oh, what a balm!
A clink of jewels, a playful jest,
Shining bright, we're at our best.

Those tiny trinkets hold our grins,
Each secret thread, where fun begins.
We twirl and spin, all pearls and flair,
Dancing shadows, without a care.

Oh, laughter rides on the evening breeze,
Adorned in mischief, we tease and please.
As light fades low, our antics soar,
A riot of jest, who could ask for more?

With each new twist, the tales unfold,
In dusk's embrace, our stories told.
We wear our secrets, bright and loud,
Under the stars, we're joyfully proud.

The Soft Luster of Memory's Palette

In hues of twilight, laughter beams,
Shining boldly in our dreams.
A shimmer here, a sparkle there,
Recalling joys that we all share.

Each little trinket, a story spun,
Underneath the fading sun.
We giggle softly as we parade,
In colors bright, our fears betrayed.

A wink of silver, a dash of gold,
Reminders of a past retold.
Every moment swirled in jest,
Crafted memories, we wear with zest.

The art of laughter paints the night,
In this soft luster, everything's right.
As time ticks on, we laugh and play,
In our treasure chest, we'll always stay.

Whispers of Midnight Elegance

At midnight's hour, elegance laughs,
With swirls of glitter on our drafts.
We twinkling gems in shadows hide,
Where whispers and giggles collide.

A crooked pin and a cheeky tone,
Transform the night into our own.
Each flicker of light, a playful wink,
Our humor flows, we barely think.

Dressed in jest, we roam the streets,
With jeweled echoes, laughter repeats.
A jesting dance in the silver moon,
We're allure and fun, in perfect tune.

In elegance layered with mischief sweet,
We create our world, no need for deceit.
As whispers swirl, our minds take flight,
Bound by the magic of the night.

Gems of the Night Whisper

Under starlit skies, we gather round,
With gems of laughter, joy abounds.
Each shiny trinket, a silly grace,
In the dark, we find our place.

A sparkle here and a giggle there,
Handcrafted moments in the air.
We flirt with dreams, empty and bright,
In the theater of our delight.

With every jest, we lace our prose,
Stealing the show, as laughter grows.
Each gem a whisper, soft and sly,
In midnight's glow, we soar and fly.

As secrets dance on the gentle breeze,
We twine our fate with playful ease.
In the night's embrace, our spirits sing,
With gems and giggles, we're everything.

A Treasure Lost in the Quiet Night

In a pocket deep, a gem laid low,
Twinkling bright where no one can go.
The cat in the corner, with a knowing grin,
Wonders quite loudly where to begin.

Did the dog swallow it? Or was it the flea?
We search high and low, while sipping our tea.
The mice hold their laughter, it's a party of fun,
While we chase shadows, thinking we've won.

In the cupboard under, a treasure may hide,
Wrapped up in old socks, with gold on the side.
We stumble and fumble, our dignity lost,
But finding the humor, well that's worth the cost.

So we laugh at the chaos, a hunt of great cheer,
For what's lost in the night, could just reappear.
With a wink from the cat, and a cheer from the mice,
Let's toast to the missing! What a great slice!

The Enigmatic Beauty of the Concealed

A dainty thing hidden, a tale yet to spin,
It's lost in the shadows, where we search to begin.
With a chuckle and nudge, the secrets will rise,
Like the smell of warm cookies, oh such a surprise!

Under blankets of dust, it sneezed with a squeak,
As the raccoon outside gave a mischievous peek.
We scour the attic, the basement, all rooms,
Dodging old memories, while laughter resumes.

The chime of the laughter marks what we seek,
A button, a thimble, but never a peak.
Is it lost or forgotten, just waiting for light?
Even in shadows, it dances with delight.

A hidden surprise, wrapped in old lace,
Adventures in finding, a comical chase.
For treasures aren't diamonds, but moments to share,
With giggles and joy, and a sprinkle of flair.

Moonlit Memories in the Dark

In the glow of the moon, where mischief takes flight,
A glimmer of laughter dances through the night.
A squirrel with swagger, on a moonbeam it prances,
While shadows hold secrets of whimsical glances.

Beneath starry skies, where giggles ignite,
We unearth the past, with sheer pure delight.
A rubber band ball, a sock with a tale,
Compose our adventures, not fancy nor frail.

An odd little trinket, a wonderfully strange,
With each twist and turn, a moment we change.
The echoes of laughter blend in with the dark,
Transforming the night into a whimsical spark.

So we chase after memories, sweet lemony zest,
Finding joy in the shadows, and laughter's the best.
What's lost isn't gone, it's a game we now play,
Under the moonlight, our whims lead the way.

Shrouded Whispers of Elegance

In silence it whispers, through cobwebbed grace,
An elegance hidden, with a mischievous face.
A vase leaning lonely, on a rickety shelf,
Who knew that such beauty could giggle itself?

While forks have their dances, and spoons spin around,
The curtains keep secrets of laughter profound.
We stumble through shadows, on a quest for the glee,
Every trip a new saga, let's wait and see!

The elegance here knows a joke or two,
With each twist and turn, it's a whimsical view.
In corners it hums, a delightful refrain,
Of treasures and trinkets, lost yet gained.

So come join the laughter, let's find what we miss,
In the shroud of the night, there's a wink and a kiss.
For elegance won't be trapped, no, not even slight,
It dances with humor, in the cloak of the night.

Starlit Trinkets and Twilight Tales

In the night, a sparkly thing,
Twinkling bright, it starts to sing.
Oh! What jesters in the night,
Making shadows dance with delight.

A sapphire wink from a misplaced pin,
Whispers secrets deep within.
Who knew such mischief could reside,
In a trinket that we all abide?

Hats take flight, and shoes do sway,
As we stumble in a merry way.
Shiny sparks in every nook,
In the clutches of a rookie cook.

Here's to laughter, here's to cheer,
In every twinkle, we hold dear.
With starlit tales that lead us far,
We gather 'round beneath the stars.

Mystique of a Forgotten Keepsake

A locket lost beneath the junk,
Whispers tales of a cheerful punk.
It creaks with memories that won't leave,
Frolicsome laughs we can't believe.

A button here, a charm askew,
Dancing saucy like morning dew.
It spins with stories, oh so bold,
Of mishaps and moments, oft retold.

Poking fun at the everyday,
It gleams and giggles in ballet.
With every glance, a side-splitting jest,
In the clutter, we find our best.

So hold that keepsake close, my friend,
For it brings laughter that won't end.
In mysteries wrapped and ribbons tied,
We find our joys we cannot hide.

Captured Light in the Abyss

In shadows deep, a glimmer shines,
Tickling laughter, and sipping wines.
A pearl that leapt from a diving spree,
Riding waves of absurdity.

Foolish treasures in the gloom,
Maybe leftovers from a broom.
Who would think a lost old gem,
Could start this wild, unruly whim?

Beneath a rock, it smirks and beams,
Like a jester caught in dreams.
Lighting up the darkest night,
With every shine, it sparks delight.

So here's to blunders and silly finds,
Laughter echoes in our minds.
In absurd combos, life's a part,
With captured light that warms the heart.

A Glint of Time's Requiem

A vintage clasp from days of yore,
Winks at us from the dusty floor.
Ticking softly, it jokes with time,
In funny rhythms, such a rhyme.

Old memories stuck in laughter's loop,
Dancing wildly in the soup.
Each glint brings giggles, no need for woe,
As time plays games, in fun and glow.

It once held keys to something grand,
Now just tickles, a merry band.
With every sparkle, a jest unfolds,
As we laugh at the tales it holds.

So hold that glint and share a laugh,
In silly moments, we find our path.
Time may tick, but joy remains,
In forgotten trinkets, life refrains.

Shimmering Secrets Beneath Shadows

In shadows where whispers of secrets lie,
A glimmering treasure catches the eye,
With chuckles and giggles, it starts to play,
Twinkling so bright, it leads us astray.

The cat in the corner gives quite the stare,
Wondering why humans dance without care,
Though the night is dark, spirits are high,
For laughter is the light that will never die.

A tap on the shoulder, a wink in the night,
The sparkle winks back, oh what a sight!
It shimmies and shakes in a humorous way,
Inviting us all to join in the fray.

Under the moonlight, we're all dressed in cheer,
With twinkling delights that bring us near,
This secret we share, a riot in sight,
Who knew joy could shimmer so vividly bright?

The Hidden Spark in Twilight

In twilight's embrace, a giggle is heard,
A spark in the gloom, oh how absurd!
It dances and flickers, just out of reach,
Teasing our senses, like a curious peach.

The socks on the line, a comical sight,
Swirl in the breezes, a humorous flight,
A flash of delight, like fireflies roam,
In the laughter of shadows, we find our home.

As children of dusk, we ponder the rhyme,
Of jesters and jest, in the twilight's prime,
A glimmer of mischief, with a wink and a nod,
Promising chuckles, no need for a facade.

Come join the glee 'neath the indigo sky,
Where giggles and grins make the heart fly,
We'll cherish the spark, in shadows so grand,
As humor unites us, hand in hand.

A Glint Amongst the Gloom

Through the murky dimness, a glint starts to shine,
An odd little bauble, not yours but not mine,
It jumps with a twitch and it dances the night,
In the midst of our giggles, it offers delight.

The fridge starts to hum, a ticklish tease,
While crumbs on the floor plead for a squeeze,
It rolls and it tumbles, a mischievous spark,
No worries at all, in this whimsical dark.

A creature scuttles, what could it be?
Just friends having fun, can't you see?
They sparkle and clamor, they play with flair,
In every shadow, the laughter's laid bare.

As the night slowly fades, the humor turns bright,
Underneath the moon's gaze, what a splendid sight!
With a glint and a giggle, we wander away,
For laughter, dear friend, is the glow of the day.

Enchantment Adorned in Silence

In silence, it twinkles, oh what a charm,
A whimsical vibe, it brings no alarm,
Who knew that in quiet, such ruckus could lie,
A sparkling delight that can make spirits fly?

The clock on the wall starts to wobble and sway,
Telling tall tales of a magical play,
A feathered friend chirps from the back of the room,
With jokes up its sleeve, it dispels all the gloom.

So stop for a moment, breathe in the peace,
Let laughter surround you, may it never cease,
For in the hush of the night, a joy takes its flight,
With sparkling enchantments to brighten our sight.

A tiptoe of laughter, a shimmer of glee,
Wrapped softly in silence, together we're free,
With flickering giggles, a playful delight,
We'll dance in the echoes of this quiet night.

Glimmers of Forgotten Elegance

In the drawer they gather dust,
Lost treasures, oh how they rust!
Yet when the moon shines bright,
They twinkle with such delight!

Once they danced at fancy balls,
Now they hide in darkened halls.
A squirrel in a tuxedo,
Adorning pine with style, you know!

With mismatched gems and colors bold,
Stories linger, waiting to be told.
Every shiny piece holds a tale,
Of laughter, mishaps, and a cat's wail!

So gather those trinkets from the past,
Dust them off, make beauty last.
In every shimmer, there's a chuckle,
A legacy wrapped in a cozy snuggle!

Secret Adornments in Shadow

In shadows deep, they come alive,
Dancing dreams that twist and dive.
A mismatched pair, a sparkly shoe,
Telling secrets we never knew!

A ribbon lost from Grandma's hair,
Swirls about in midnight air.
Glances shared in the moon's embrace,
Giggling gems in a playful chase!

With every blink, they shine and shine,
Clowns in costumes, oh so divine!
Forgotten pearls in a mess so grand,
Whirling tales at their command!

In corners dark, they hold their glee,
Adventurers in a land so free.
So let them whisper, let them shout,
Funny jewels, here's what they're about!

The Heirloom's Whisper

Whispers soft from times of yore,
A locket that could tell much more.
Tickled pink with each clink and clank,
A jester's laugh in a silver plank!

Caught in webs of cobweb dust,
Got lost in nostalgia and trust.
Fabulous faux gems, a cheeky glance,
Winks and nudges in a daring dance!

Ribbons tangled, oh what a sight,
Silken stories darting in the night.
What to wear? A rubber band?
Elegance folded with a clown's hand!

So lift the lid on grandma's chest,
Let history reveal its jest.
Joyful trinkets, laughter on the way,
Shimmering anecdotes come out to play!

Midnight Sparkles on Fabric

Underneath the midnight sky,
Twirling beads go zooming by.
A rogue diamond in a sock,
Sending everyone into shock!

Silk and satin, oh what a tease,
A crow's feather brings you to your knees.
Mismatched buttons telling a joke,
A jacket's secret in the cloak!

With laughter stitched in every thread,
A funky pattern full of dread.
Cuddly shapes that dare to prance,
Together in a quirky dance!

So cuddle up with style so bold,
Worn with whimsy, a sight to behold.
Midnight sparkles on every seam,
Funny tales wrapped in a dream!

The Shimmering Veil of Night

In shadows where creatures play,
A sparkle winks in a sly way,
It teases the dreams that drift high,
As giggles dance from the dark sky.

A glow sticks out from the gloom,
Like a misplaced flower in bloom,
It beckons with whispers so sweet,
While critters shuffle on tiny feet.

A twinkle here, a flicker there,
Like fireflies caught without a care,
What secrets lie beneath its grace?
We giggle, puzzled by the place.

With mischief draped like a fine lace,
The night reveals a funny face,
In the depths of midnight's thrall,
We share a laugh; we're having a ball.

Holding Beauty in the Abyss

In the depths where oddities thrive,
A wonder that's cheeky, alive,
It twirls in the dark with a wink,
Making us laugh more than we think.

Amidst the creatures of the night,
Lies a gem that shines just right,
It murmurs jokes in a hushed tone,
As we admire its sparkly throne.

A mishap with spooky flair,
It lights up the night, the perfect pair,
With shadows that giggle and dance,
We lose ourselves to a frolicsome chance.

What treasures hide in this delight?
They dance through dreams, oh what a sight!
Caught in laughter and cosmic bliss,
We explore the beauty we dare not miss.

Secrets of the Twilight Trinket

A trinket glows with a charming spark,
Hiding secrets within the dark,
It teeters on the edge of night,
While shadows play in the moonlight.

We whisper and giggle in glee,
As the darkness reveals its spree,
With every twist and curious turn,
A funny riddle we all discern.

Why does it shimmer with such a grin?
It knows the fun that lies within,
Cackles erupt from the sleepy earth,
Where laughter blooms in the silent mirth.

As we gather in its quirky charm,
In the twilight, there's no alarm,
We romp and tumble in joyous song,
In the secrets where we all belong.

The Unseen Elegance of Darkness

An elegance wrapped in night's arms,
Flashes of humor with subtle charms,
In the dark an unexpected jest,
We giggle soft, forgetting the rest.

From unseen corners, echoes tease,
The dark reveals peculiar keys,
With every giggle, shadows prance,
Inviting us all to join the dance.

What lovely oddities come alive,
In the dark where silliness thrives,
Their whispers tickle like a breeze,
Spreading joy like a laughing freeze.

A nocturnal laughter fills the air,
While elegance hides in a playful dare,
We circle 'round in the nighttime glow,
Finding humor in what we don't know.

Radiant Memories Off the Beaten Path

In the attic I found an old hat,
With feathers and sparkles, imagine that!
A time-travel cap to whimsically wear,
Turns you into laughter, everywhere.

The mirror reflects a peculiar sight,
A polka-dot suit that's far from bright.
With mismatched shoes and a wink of glee,
I danced like a squirrel, wild and free.

Jellybean colors, a riot of hue,
A crazy ensemble, what would you do?
With each twirl and twist, the past skips forth,
Mocking my style, so full of mirth.

So, let's celebrate with a day of cheer,
Dressing awfully strange brings fun near.
In radiant memories, we laugh and sway,
Finding joy in our quirky display.

Hidden Glamour in the Night

Out in the garden, the gnomes stand tall,
With sparkly capes, they're ready to brawl!
A disco ball hangs in the moonlit air,
As they boogie and twirl without a care.

Under the stars, they steal the scene,
Sporting wild hats in colors obscene.
With plastic forks, they dance like pros,
Their silly moves, the best kind of shows.

A hidden glamour, oh what a view,
As tinsel trees dance to the quirky tune.
Each twinkle and shimmer brings giggles galore,
With laughter ringing from each garden store.

So join the gnomes in their midnight spree,
With glittering smiles, so cheerful and free.
Under the night sky, let worries fall,
In hidden glamour, let giggles enthrall.

Glimpse of Gold in the Dark

Digging through junk, what could I find?
A snazzy old locket, of a curious kind.
But clasped in my fingers was nothing but air,
An empty medal? A prank, I declare!

Yet in the shadows, a glimmering grace,
A rubber chicken wearing a crown on its face.
With nonsensical charm, it perched on the shelf,
Inviting us all to just be ourselves.

The gold that I sought in the depths of the night,
Turned out to be something awfully bright.
So I laugh with the chicken, my new scepter divine,
In ridiculous moments, our joy intertwines.

Who knew that the dark had a twist so absurd?
With rubbery wisdom, it's heard but preferred.
In bursts of delight, with the chicken I walk,
Shining in shadows, our silly sweet talk.

Shimmering Tales of Yesteryear

Dust off the trunk, tales come alive,
With sparkling jewels, where oddities thrive.
A hat with a feather that wiggles and sways,
And mismatched socks telling wild stories of days.

In shimmering tales, the past comes to play,
With polka-dot dinosaurs leading the way.
They chat and they gossip, all wrinkled with cheer,
As laughter echoes, our worries disappear.

An old pair of shades, so funky and bright,
Worn in a time where the world felt just right.
Throw in a dance move that never quite lands,
And sprinkle some giggles like glitter from hands.

So here's to the treasures we've tucked away tight,
The quirks and the laughs that roll through the night.
In shimmering stories, let's waltz with delight,
Finding magic in nonsense, all hearts shining bright.

Midnight's Crowning Mystery

In shadows deep, where gags do dwell,
A crafty thief has tales to tell.
With sparkly things, they prance about,
Count the shiny gems, then shout!

Whispers float like jests at play,
In corners where lost trinkets stay.
A dance of light, what's that I see?
A laughing sprite? Oh, it's just me!

Through velvet night, the mischief blooms,
As wobbling cups spill all the tunes.
What's this delight that twinkles high?
A jesting rogue who steals the pie!

As dawn approaches, all's a whirl,
The night still giggles, that sneaky pearl.
Each curious find, a cheerful tease,
Bright laughter echoes in the breeze.

An Obscured Treasure Revealed

Behind the curtain, something's neat,
A little box with an enticing treat.
What's tucked inside? A riddle fair,
With giggles and gags beyond compare.

A jeweled wink from a hidden grin,
Let's solve this puzzle, dive right in!
The clues are scattered, oh what a mess,
A pair of socks? Or maybe a dress?

With each wild guess, the laughter grows,
Is that a ring or an artful nose?
A treasure found under glitter and foam,
Turns out it's just a rubbery gnome!

In daylight's peek, the truth is clear,
That treasure gained comes with good cheer.
Each silly thing brought out to play,
Is just the joy of a funny day!

Reflections of Dusk's Embrace

As the sun dips low, a chuckle rings,
The night wears laughter, and mischief sings.
In twilight's hug, what fun we find,
Silly whispers drift, unconfined.

Through the glimmering haze, shadows dance,
A round of jest with a goofy prance.
Fluffy kittens chase the stars,
Could they join us? Yes, how bizarre!

With each twinkling gleam in sight,
The moon joins in with pure delight.
Nonsense glows in evening's flight,
Making even the silence feel bright.

So grab a tale from the dusky grin,
Join the twilight, feel the spin.
As laughter bubbles in the night air,
Each reflective giggle turns into flair.

A Glimmering Memory of Secrets

In the attic's gloom, where secrets lie,
A glint of gold catches the eye.
Mysterious charms from years gone by,
With tales untold that seem to sigh.

A spinning top with a crooked toss,
An eraser shaped like a tiny boss!
Laughter echoes through dusty halls,
As we unearth these jolly thralls.

Every odd find wrapped tight in lore,
Brings back the chuckles, forevermore.
An old shoe horn? What a curious prize!
It held the secrets of laughing lies!

As we rummage through this timeworn chest,
The joy of memories is truly the best.
Each shining trinket, a ticket to glee,
A celebration of whimsy, you see!

The Radiant Silence Unveiled

In the quiet of night, a twinkle shines,
A sneaky little gem, with mischief entwined.
It whispers to shadows, a dance so bright,
"Join me in laughter, beneath the moonlight!"

With a giggle it glistens, oh what a show,
It tickles the stars, putting on quite a glow.
A charm from the heavens, alive with glee,
In a cloak of the dark, how silly can we be!

Underneath all the laughter, a secret concealed,
A treasure in jest, and joy is revealed.
Each glimmer and sparkle, a trickery bold,
In the quiet of night, a fun tale unfolds!

As we frolic together, no worries to find,
That gem in the shadows, it dances, unbind.
A riot of color, a playful delight,
In the silence of night, it brings such a light.

Adornments of the Night's Melody

In the cloak of the night, where whispers reside,
A wink from the darkness, that spark can't hide.
It tickles the echoes, with humor and flair,
Crafted from starlight, it floats through the air.

Poking fun at the quiet, with glimmers that dance,
It sways with each chuckle, a night-time romance.
A melody forming, in hues oh so bright,
Singing to shadows, like laughter takes flight.

With a flicker it jests, and the darkness grins wide,
As we waltz with the dreams, letting joy be our guide.
In this jolly parade, where glories unite,
We wear all the giggles, adorned by the night.

Each sparkle's a story, a jest in the gloom,
In the heart of the dark, together we bloom.
So gather your chuckles, and let flares embark,
For the night's playful dress is a whimsical spark!

Fragments of Light in Deep Shadows

In the depths of the night, where shadows do play,
A sparkle of mischief brightens the way.
Tiny bits of laughter, like stars on a spree,
Each flicker a giggle, so wild and free!

They tumble and bounce, like sprites in a game,
Contriving sly antics, never feeling the shame.
In the quiet of dark, where chuckles collide,
A bit of pure magic begins to abide.

With every small twinkle, a chuckle takes flight,
Each shimmer a jest that ignites in the night.
Fragments of fun weave a tapestry bright,
A twinkling reminder that joy's our birthright!

So let's roam together, through shadows galore,
As light-hearted fragments start to explore.
In the depths of our laughter, we linger and spark,
Finding sweet joy in a world full of dark.

A Dazzling Shadow's Tale

There once was a shadow, both quirky and spry,
With iridescent dreams and a glimmering eye.
It pranced through the twilight, wearing pure glee,
With tales of adventure, for you and for me!

In the silence it shimmied, making shadows dance,
Tickling the stars, daring night to prance.
From corners of darkness, it shouted with cheer,
"Come join in my frolic, for laughter is here!"

With a skip and a twirl, it leaped through the gloom,
A dizzy delight in the night's quiet room.
From the depth of the dark, a giggling parade,
Each flicker of light, a new yarn to cascade!

So here's to the stories, of shadows and spark,
In the heart of the night where we play in the dark.
With each twinkle and chuckle, let freely prevail,
The dazzling adventure of a shadow's bright tale!

The Secret Lace of Shadowy Splendor

In twilight's cloak, a dance begins,
The cats wear socks, while laughter spins.
A sneaky wink from a cheeky sprite,
Whispers tickle the edge of night.

Beneath the stars, a sock parade,
Where shadows jig and play charades.
A glance of glitter, a twinkle bright,
Socks and secrets, oh what a sight!

Mysteries Embedded in Silken Depths

In silken folds, a riddle hides,
A butterfly with mismatched sides.
It flutters round, a giggling ghost,
Wearing stripes like a fancy host.

A teapot's laugh, a spoon's delight,
With tales that twirl in the darkest night.
Their tales unfold with every sip,
As shadows dance and shadows trip.

A Tale Wrought with Dusk's Trimmings

When daylight fades, the fun ignites,
As shoes take flight on whimsical nights.
With every step, a chuckle brews,
In darkness' arms, we chase our shoes.

A wandering hat with dreams of tea,
Sips invisible, just you and me.
With winks and giggles, we roam the dark,
Finding treasures in a silk-threaded park.

The Elegance Embedded in Gloom

In shadows deep, a jester grins,
Tickling fancies as the night begins.
With whiskers bright and a jaunty flair,
Dancing socks float without a care.

Beneath the moon, secrets confide,
As laughter echoes, and fears subside.
With every twirl, a story gleams,
In the gloom, we live our dreams.

www.ingramcontent.com/pod-product-compliance
Lightning Source LLC
Chambersburg PA
CBHW060124230426
43661CB00003B/322